Our Common Life:

REFLECTIONS ON
BEING A SPOUSE

ॐ

by Mary and Rob
Glover

In memory of our parents:
Fay and Viola Glover
&
Ed and Nellie Naughton

Living the Good News, Inc.

a division of The Morehouse Publishing Group

Editorial Offices
600 Grant Street, Suite 400
Denver, CO 80203

Cover Design and Layout: Val Price

Printed in the United States of America.

The scripture quotations used within are from the New
Revised Standard Version Bible, copyright © 1989 by the
Division of Christian Education of the National Council of
Churches of Christ in the U.S.A. Used by permission.

ISBN 1-889108-23-5

Foreword

Couples who live in committed relationships in the world today are a very important sign of God's creative, redemptive and sustaining love for the world. This book of reflections is written to encourage all of those spouses to continue to work at their loving relationships.

The two of us hope this book will be a simple tool for partners—one that can be used for a brief moment of reflection by either person, individually or together. It might find a home in the bedroom, bathroom, car or wherever a few moments can be found to reflect on your spiritual journey as a couple.

We are a normal couple—we love each other, we like each other and sometimes we can't stand each other! We have found in our relationship that we often do not communicate with one another enough, be it through talking, writing, touching or smiling. We hope these affirmations might help couples to communicate in their relationship and to reflect on their holy partnership. They may help you express some of the things you experience and feel.

When we began this project, we were unsure at times that we could even find one affirmation, let alone dozens of them. We thought a book of condemnations might be easier! But once we moved beyond that, we realized how important it is to look for the blessings, take stock of our gifts and affirm the good that is around and about us in our daily living.

We live in a household of eight, the two of us and six growing children between the ages of 7 and 16. The first miracle is that we found time to write down any of these thoughts. The laundry didn't always get done, but then it never does, and we even found an affirmation or two about that.

The second miracle is that we ourselves

have benefitted from and enjoyed the process. We discovered that a good way to communicate is to write short comments about various moments of our day and then share them with each other.

May each of your moments as individuals in partnership be times of blessing for you.

"Dear friend, we are sea and land.

It is not our purpose to become each other—

it is to recognize each other—

to learn to see the other and honor him for what he is—

each the other's opposite and complement."

—*Hermann Hesse*

☙❧

Fireworks and Fireflies

On our way to see the Fourth of July fireworks, we saw fireflies dancing on the path. Just like kids, we caught them in a jar and brought some home to hold in our hands. The fireworks were loud and colorful, spectacular and exciting, but they didn't overshadow the fireflies. The fireflies filled us with wonder and awe. They stayed with us and mysteriously lit the night around us on our way home. The joy in our relationship sometimes comes in loud colorful flashes and sometimes in a gentle winking glow.

Our love is fireworks and fireflies.

Busy Life

There is always too much to do—too much that needs to be done—that bill to be paid, those errands to run, drop off those videos, pick up those groceries. But did I stop today to make sure you are still there? Did I look in your eyes to see the person I love? If I take one moment to think what makes my life a treasure to me, you come to mind. One shared smile makes me realize that we are in this together, and I enjoy being busy if you are there, working beside me.

God, thank you for giving us
each other in this busy life.

Nice Work!

This special relationship that I live with my spouse is such an important part of my life. I will take time to talk and play with my spouse, to nurture our love. Even when I can't stand anymore of his or her stupid habits, I will continue to live through them, taking the time to be with my spouse. After all, relationships were never meant to be easy; even Adam and Eve had a little trouble working together! How sincere and deep can love be when we aren't forced to love through the pain and strife, too? Love is no easy street; it is downright hard work.

> "*Holding hands at midnight*
> *'neath a starry sky,*
>
> *nice work if you can get it,*
> *and you can get it if you try.*"

(Ira Gershwin)

Did I Forget?

You were leaving. We were tied up with the hustle of getting ready, did I forget to say I love you? Doing the laundry and packing the clothes, did I forget to say I love you? The last minute rush to get the workshops ready and the copies made, did I forget to say I love you? Going to the bank and getting to the airport, did I forget to say I love you? Probably.

I love you!

Impatience

I wanted those bills paid yesterday and that project finished last week. I get so tired of waiting, waiting and waiting, God. Will these things ever get completed? Oh yes, I know it took seven days to make the world and Rome was not built in a day. And I know this house took a year to build, and our relationship didn't just happen. Come to think of it, it took nine months to get me breathing in this world. Okay, I get the message, God!

Please help me be a patient person
of prayer who perseveres.

Treehouse

It's my dream house. It was when I was a child and it is now when I'm an adult. And some think I built it for my children! I can still remember the vivid pictures of *Swiss Family Robinson*, running water and all. The joy for me is sitting in it and letting the rest of the world rush by me. I am in the cool shade of the leaves and the wind gently blows across my face. What more could I ask for? There she is, climbing the stairs to our treehouse.

Thank you, God, for my wife
to share my treehouse.

Balance

I can live a balanced life by allowing myself time to rest and enjoy the moment. This Twentieth Century of the working man and woman and our struggle for more power, fame and wealth has done its damage to our health and happiness. We know our worth is not found in money, job or position, but so often we live by those worldly principles and forget that we are worthy just because we are a child of God.

I will take time today to remember that I am a child of God, created for rest and enjoyment just as much as for toil and labor.

વ્&

Living in the Mess

Being a perfectionist is never easy, and little by little I am learning to let go of some things. I am learning to walk around and through rooms that need to be picked up or need cleaning. I am slowly accepting the truth that my relationship with my spouse and my children is more important than having a perfectly cleaned and kept house. I can even go to bed with dirty dishes in the kitchen! My mother may not have allowed it, but I don't think you mind, do you, God?

> "You make the bed, you do the
> dishes and six months later you
> have to start all over again."
>
> (J. Rivers)

God of Chaos, be with us in this holy mess!

Talk—Touch

"I love your hand on my back. I could lay here all day with you scratching my head." These words of touch affirmation between couples are so important for us to do, to hear and to say to one another. All too often we experience something the other has done and fail to make a response. Communicating with one another is so very important for us whether it is talking about touching one another or just sharing struggles of the day.

Dear God, help us to verbalize
our thoughts, feelings and
emotions with one another
when they happen.

ღ

Laughter

That person seems to wear a smile on her face all the time. How can she be so happy all the time? Some days it seems that I don't even have a happy thought. But today I am going to recover the gift of laughter and happiness. Despite all the traffic and the deadlines, sometime in this busy day of mine there will be something that happens that will call for a laugh or a smile and this time that laugh or smile is going to come from me!

"He who laughs, lasts."

(Anonymous)

Thank you, God, for the gift of laughter
—it does wonders for my soul.

Hop Over It

It is a phrase that makes all of us laugh, especially when we say it to our children. Each of us gets so caught up in our own hot issues and aggravations that we can seldom see anything but the problem. Today, when I am faced with a frustrating situation, I am going to tell myself (not my children) to "hop over it." And I *can* hop over it and then I will be much happier and healthier for it!

Hop over it, hop over it!

Laundry Finished

I've heard a lot of people say, "I stopped everything else today and just did laundry. I wanted to get it all finished." I can certainly understand that. I want to see that job completed, accomplished, over, finished. Those same people always end the story with, "When the last load was in the dryer they all came home and changed clothes," or, "Just as it was all finished I spilled something all over my shirt." I can just see the piles of laundry growing right before their eyes. Maybe our experiences with laundry can teach us to rejoice in the process and not in the ending.

Thanks for being my spouse in
this process of growing a relationship,
another job never finished. I find
excitement and joy in the work.

Laundry Process

We can rejoice in the process, not in the completion. That is a lesson we need in many parts of life, especially in our relationship. I know we don't want our relationship to be finished and out of the way like the laundry, but we do often want it to be set, static, something we can step back and look at and say, "We have a good relationship." But one of us is always throwing another shirt or towel in the basket! I always have one new quirk for you to live with or you always have one more expectation I didn't recognize. Let's try to rejoice in the process. We are blessed to have the chance to live day-to-day with each other, to rearrange our relationship each day in a new way.

Be with us, God,
in this never-ending process.

Rearranging Again

I love to rearrange rooms, furniture, books and knick-knacks because it gives a fresh and different look to a room and the things within it. Besides, it forces us to dust, vacuum and sort piles of stuff that have become like immovable fixtures. Change can be a good thing at home and at work and within myself. It gives me a new way to look at the world. It helps me re-examine those fixed things that may need to be put away or may just need a little dusting.

With God's help, I will make some change in my life today...

Together—Apart

How can I love her when I can hardly stand to be around her? Is there something wrong with me when I have days that my wife drives me nuts? I used to think there was something wrong with me, but now I think that I am very normal. It is not easy to live together, to be so completely intimate, to be life spouses. (It was certainly not all wine and roses on Noah's Ark either.) So, I guess I can accept the days when I want to be divorced and miles away from her. It is natural to feel this way at times. The details of life always get messy and sticky. So I can give myself some space, some time apart. And my wife will appreciate it, too, I bet!

God, help us to value our time
together…and our time apart!

Infatuation

Even after all these years, sometimes I look at you and my heart beats funny and my skin gets warm and tingly. It feels like that breath-stealing crush I had in high school. I wonder if I tried to talk to you, if I'd blush and stammer. I'm happy that most of the time we are comfortable with each other. I feel the warm and steady love that comes after time together, but it's also great that sometimes my heart can leap and do somersaults at the sight of you.

I look at you across the room
and I am "in love." Thanks for the thrill!

God Grant Me

Wisdom and serenity are gifts I pray for often. I always want to change the people around me—my spouse, my boss, my neighbors. I know exactly what's wrong with them and what they could do to improve themselves! But I continue to learn from experience that they are exactly the ones I cannot change! Yes, but something has got to change—I can't stand the way things are now! I so much want change, except when it comes to changing myself, my opinions, my habits, my mode of operation. Of course that is exactly the only thing I can change, with the help of God. Dear God, please give me loads of courage!

Today I will change one little thing
about myself that could be better.
Nothing more—nothing less!

Proud

I have the greatest spot to sit back and watch. The world is trying to drive you crazy. It throws one obstacle in your path and you lightly step around it, another and you leap right over it. You are in the midst of commotion and turmoil but you are calm and steady, moving forward toward the goal. People say to me, "He is amazing! Doesn't anything phase him?" And I proudly say, "He handles it well."

I am so proud of you. Thank God for your abilities and persistence.

Miss You

I know it's only a few days, a little bit of time, but when you're gone I miss you! Of course, it is easy to miss you. You are not here to share your warmth, and I'm cold. You're not here to share my frustrating day, and have I got frustrations! I can't take you for granted when you are not here. It is easy to miss you, but not as easy to enjoy you when you are here. I'll try to be as aware of you when you're here as I am when you're gone.

God, help me to appreciate and
love my spouse whether he or
she is near or far away.

Aging

When I was a teenager I thought people in their twenties and thirties were young. Those in their forties and fifties were old and those sixty and older were just plain ancient. Now that I am in the forties-fifties bracket, I think that age group is rather young! And those in their sixties and seventies are just starting to age! It is interesting how our perceptions of others change when we become the other.

God help me not to judge others until I have walked a mile (or ten or twenty years) in their shoes. And help me grow in wisdom as I grow older.

Lord, help me grow as I age.

☯

Living and Dying

Through our living and our dying we are giving birth to the risen Lord in our lives and the lives of our children and neighbors. So what am I dying to today? How can I go on living with all of this dying, pain and suffering all around me? Some of the most alive people I meet are those who are facing death.

Today I will embrace death in the midst of my living. I will walk through, with and in the face of pain and death. The smallest and the biggest seed will not come to life unless it first goes deep into the darkened loam and gives itself over to a new kind of existence. We are all growing. We are all changing. We are all living. We are all dying.

> *"In our living and our dying we*
> *are bringing you to birth."*

(Bernadette Farrell from the song "God Beyond All Names")

Here I Am

I have been clamoring and clutching for change in my life, hope and new direction, for over a year. I've been in a mad dash, desperately running since the quiet moments found over a year ago. This quiet place near the lake could be the waters off the "Marginal Way" in Ogunquit, Maine, or it could be the quaintness and history of Boston or the soulfulness of a gurgling stream in Colorado. It matters not where, but it matters that I am here, fully, totally, present here in this place. I find joy and comfort in the grass, birds, trees, water. Here are hopes of recreation and renewal.

Here I am, O God.

Family—Friends

The attention, care and nurturing that I give to my family is the greatest gift that I can give to them. Do I really need to go out and buy another present or spend more money on them to tell them I love them? It just takes an initial step of dialing my sister's number or sitting on the couch next to my child or writing a note to my aunt, or going for a walk with my loved one.

"By letting go, it all gets done. The world is won by those who let it go!"

(Tao Te Ching)

Today I will take time for my family and friends—they are important to me, more important than any of my projects or work!

Oh, What a Beautiful Morning

Yes, I love to wake up and enjoy early mornings and my spouse loves to enjoy them by sleeping! We are such opposites in so many ways that sometimes I can hardly stand it. Do opposites really attract one another? Our differences give us opportunities and ways to cope as a couple. I can take time for my own reflection or needs in those early morning hours. I can do all of those little details now when she is sleeping so we can take advantage of our time together when we are both awake. Mornings aren't for everybody.

*Thank you, Lord, for the
beauty of the morning.*

Kitchen Kiss

One of my fond memories of childhood is coming upon my parents in the kitchen kissing. They would often be embarrassed and get busy doing something else, anything else, but sometimes my dad would purposefully hug all the harder and "Mmmmm...." just for my benefit. What a warm feeling that gave me. And what a wonderful gift we can give our family and our world.

Let them see we love each other!

ॐ

Partners—Parents

How in the world are couples able to be both spouses and parents? It is so easy to lose our relationship with each other when we pay attention to our children. We can take a few days away each year to just be spouses—no kids, no parenting. We can take a few minutes each day to just be partners, relate simply as lovers, not as care-givers or parents. The two words may have the same letters but each word needs its own time and focus!

God, help us take time to be loving
spouses, first and last.

Thank You, God

There was a second out of time tonight,
did you feel it? Did the earth shake and
the sky tremble? I was racing along just
like always when all of a sudden it
happened. I felt all the joy and blessings
that make up my life. I knew deep inside
how wonderful your presence in my life is
and I roared a heart-felt thanks for the gift
of you.

Thank you, God, for the gift of my spouse.

Grow Up!

"I wonder what I'll be when I grow up?" My spouse occasionally asks that question as we approach our mid-forties! And we laugh again at this absurd question that is full of truth. After all, now that we are grown-up with children shouldn't we know what we are? I sometimes think we have taken on the words of Peter Pan, "I'll never grow up," but, in many ways, that is so very good.

God be with us as we grow.

꘎꘎

Love Is

"Love is patient; love is kind..." So begins the familiar passage from 1 Corinthians. But lately I have often wanted to add, "Yes, and it hurts like hell at times—has anyone out there been burned lately?" The old song I used to sing in my "innocent" days of high school said, "Love hurts, love scars, it wounds and mars..." I don't think I really knew just then what I was singing about. Living in a committed relationship does take a painful amount of patience and kindness, forgiveness and forbearance. It is not just a blissful joy ride; if it is only that, it is probably not love. Love takes a lot of hard work—blood, sweat and tears.

"Trouble is part of your life, and if you don't share it, you don't give the person who loves you a chance to love you enough."

(Dinah Shore)

Electric Touch

I think there is a magic current that flows from you to me or me to you when we touch each other. Tonight when I was washing dishes you stopped and put your hand on my back. I felt that electric touch. The tensions of the day and the worries of the night flowed out of me. You are like my ground, my lightning rod, and all those buzzing emotions were drained off safely by you and replaced by calm.

Thank you, God, for my lightning rod, my ground.

ºº

Play Cards

I used to play cards only when I went home to visit my parents, and it was such fun. Just in the last few years, I've realized that card playing and games can happen in my own household as well, and it doesn't have to happen just when I am on vacation! Inviting friends over or gathering the kids together for a few games without talking business or work is a very good thing to do. It is part of that all important "holy play" time that I can make happen. I just pick up the phone and make a call. I can do it again and again.

> "Loafing needs no explanation
> and is its own excuse."
>
> (Christopher Morley)

God, help me take time to play!

We Are Tired

Oh, for just a few more hours (or minutes) of sleep! I'm so tired, and I know you are too. Life was just too full these last days and there was not enough time to sleep. This morning I can hardly pull myself out of bed. You pull me on. You are moving fast and full of energy. How can you be? I know you'll crash later when my momentum is keeping me going. You put out the energy now; I'll do it later. We are like the two old trees that lean against each other to stand. I don't think either one of us could stand on our own today.

God bless you for being a support to me.

☙❧

Simplicity

It truly is a "gift to be simple." Every time I uncomplicate my life, I am gifted. So often we over analyze, over scrutinize, over systemize or over complicate our lives. I can simplify my life. I can do less, plan less, work less. Less is more. Today I will find ways to simplify my day—to do less worrying, to do less complaining. I will schedule one or two fewer appointments and take time to sing a song or whistle a tune or go for a walk. Every time I do this I discover how really rich and full my life is. It is *simply* wonderful!

Thank you, God, for the "gift to be simple."

&

Not Like Me

You are not just like me—what a pain (and what a salvation!). You pushed me beyond myself again today. You made me realize that I knew the right thing to do and then I had to do it. This world is a better place because you are in it. Thank you, God, for the two of us with different visions and different talents. It makes life frustrating and yet it makes life whole.

Thank God you are not like me!

Enjoy Yourself

Just how do we enjoy that which we have—be it money, fame, peace, a loving relationship? It seems so often these days that we are so busy at getting ahead, keeping up with the neighbors, keeping the status quo or just keeping afloat that we don't take the time each day, each moment, to enjoy what we have. I know how precious each moment is.

Today I will take the time to enjoy each of those sacred treasures in my life—especially the various relationships in my life, whether it is my spouse, child or friend. I don't know if Ben was including anything other than money in his thoughts about wealth, but I do know that it matters not what you have, but whether you can really enjoy what it is you have in abundance.

> *"Wealth is not his who has it,*
> *but his who enjoys it."*

(Benjamin Franklin)

Fruits and Vegetables

I remember walking into my parents' house. They were sitting at their table eating a meal of fresh fruits and vegetables from their garden—raspberries, strawberries, sweet corn, tomatoes, green beans, peas, rhubarb, asparagus, lettuce. The two of them were happy to see us, of course, but they were happy before we came too. They were enjoying the fruits of their labor, their garden and us—an old couple, enjoying life together. They were tired, but happy.

God, help us to enjoy the fruits
(and vegetables) of our labors
today and in the future.

ᘒᘒ

Alarm Clock

There it goes again! Where is that snooze button? The jarring sound of the alarm clock early in the morning begins the daily ritual. Then I have the short blissful minutes to sink back under the warm covers and really enjoy sleeping. Isn't this bed wonderful? Isn't it soft and rejuvenating?

There are days that are like the alarm clock in our relationship, loud and jarring, but they just wake us up so that we can snuggle back in and really be aware of our relationship. Isn't it wonderful, warm and rejuvenating?

Thank you, God, for our marriage.

Feet

If Christians need to wash one another's feet, certainly those couples committed in lasting love need to wash one another's feet. Being of loving service and care for your spouse is the pinnacle of a loving relationship. Take time at least three or four times a year to actually wash your loved one's feet. Use soothing oils, soaps and fresh warm water. Don't be in a hurry. Caress each foot with all your love and attention. This is your beloved. This is the one with whom you can be most intimate.

For the gift of touch, we give you thanks.

Time with You

"Just give me some time with you alone, without work or the kids or meetings! I need some quality time with you today." These are words of a spouse crying for time and attention. How often we fail to spend time with the one who is most important in our life. Today I will call my spouse and set up time away from work and kids, school and church. It will be time for the one I love.

God, help me to do this again and again!

My Body

This body is a gift from God. I will feed and nurture it, bathe and clothe it. It will embrace pleasure and pain, play and work. I will stretch, strengthen and exercise its muscle, sinew and fiber. It is the temple of the Holy Spirit. The one whom I love is a gift from God—body, mind, spirit and voice. My spouse's body is also a gift from God. We have vowed to share all that we are. This is my body given over for you. This is my blood shed for you. Yes, we share our life blood in pleasure and pain, in play and work.

"Body, mind, spirit, voice, it takes the whole person to sing and rejoice."

(Helen Kemp)

My Mind

This mind of mine and the mind of my spouse are such mystery, power, bliss and confusion all at once, day in and day out. I can calm my mind, dream with my mind, exercise my mind, renew my mind, by fireside, on walks, while traveling, by streams of living water, by gentle breeze and gusting winds, by digging in rich, black soil or sandy shores or climbing rocks of barren earth. Today I will celebrate this incredible computer of my mind and of my spouse's, in busy and quiet ways.

"Bless us this day, great Spirit of Love,
bless us with life and love.
Come intertwine our pathways to you."

(R.G. from the song "Bless Us This Day")

Cooking

We share the cooking responsibilities so that when one of us can't face another decision, the other one is there at the stove. Our culinary creations are not always so marvelous, and we certainly run out of new ideas for meals, but we do take turns. It is what we need to do with all of our many household chores—take turns. This week I can take my turn at cooking, cleaning and even laundry!

God, help us to share our chores daily.

All the Joy

How can I forget all the joy that is mine today, this moment? It is immense and powerful, but then I wake up to another day and the joy is all gone, there is no sunshine. Where could it have all gone? I thought I had an endless supply! The reality is that joy and sorrow, ecstasy and pain are all part of the same highway of life. We just need to keep travelin' on and stop to smell the roses when we can!

God, be with us on this highway of life.

Work

Am I married to my work or to my spouse?
Who am I without my job? Is my value
and worth determined by how much
money I make at my job? These questions
and others surface every once in a while
for us. They are tough, but good questions.
I can take some time to write more questions and comments about my work and
my self. I can set up an appointment with
a counselor or spiritual director to help me
focus on my growth and self-worth beyond
a job. I am worthy not because of a job or
what I do.

I am God's work of art.

Crucial

Why do the most essential and crucial jobs pay little or nothing and offer few benefits? I think of my spouse's jobs—housework, child care, laundry worker, chauffeur of kids, house manager, homework tutor. No one, including the IRS, gives credit or monetary value to all of those full-time jobs. I find them of the greatest value and worth. I will take on those jobs willingly and share their responsibilities with my spouse. This work is crucial, too, though the pay is just lousy!

Lord, help us to live with
all these endless jobs.

Reality

It is hard accepting my reality. I escape from it through money, through dreaming about future possibilities, through longing for the past, good old days, through eating and sleeping. But the truth is I am not in the past and I am not in the future. I am not younger. I am not 100 pounds lighter—or even 50 or 25 pounds lighter. I don't have money to build a new house or buy a new car. I don't have money to build a new shower or renovate our kitchen or sand our floors or paint the house or buy new carpet or rugs or shades or drapes. There is a lot I don't have and will not have when I fall asleep tonight.

God, help me to accept my reality.

Counting My Blessings

So what is worth living for? Why do I keep going! What do I have? I have a wonderful gift of making music with my hands, feet, voice, ears. I have a kind, caring, companion—a marriage partner who is always there for me. I have a car that works. I have a warm house with beds, television, running water, hot showers, guitar, piano, computer. I have enough money to buy food, travel, entertainment.

I have absolutely glorious children who challenge and nurture me with love. I have a deep, mysterious faith, belief in God and in Church. I have a variety of income sources—jobs that have variety and flexibility that allow me to travel and observe others. I have siblings who are there to talk with and visit whenever I call. I have friends and associates. I have a yard to play in.

"At work, you think of the children you have left at home. At home you think of the work you have left unfinished. Such a struggle is unleashed within yourself. Your heart is rent."

(Golda Meir)

God, help me to take stock of my life and count my many blessings.

You Smell Good

My sense of smell is aroused by your aroma. There is no one else that can smell as good as you do. It must be the lotion that you put on after showering that makes me purr! When I am away from you I forget your smell, but the moment you come near, my nose seeks you out.

Thank you, God, for the gift of our senses, especially the sense of smell.

Birthdays

We all grow older, one day at a time, moment by moment. Whether we grow or wither becomes our choice of life or death. We say yes to life when we accept the moment for what it is—pain, tension or pleasure—and then offer a prayer of thanks for awareness. When we fail to grow we fail to live life fully. Another birthday is another opportunity to celebrate the joy of growing richer by the moment.

> *For another moment to live*
> *and to grow, I am grateful.*

Blizzard

Wow! The weather is horrible out there today. It hurts to breathe. The snow is blowing and the wind is howling. But it is so different here inside—just right, just right, just right! I can relax. I don't have to keep my shoulders hunched against the wind or my hands clenched so my fingers won't freeze. I can take a deep breath and my lungs don't scream with pain. You are my safe haven from the blizzard of the world! With you I can relax and take a deep breath. You are just right, just right, just right!

Thank you, God, for the people
who are safety in the storms of life.

Reading

Reading for ten minutes or five hours is a precious gift of time to give myself and my spouse. It really is soul food! I can read a newspaper, the funnies, a novel, a self-help book...it really doesn't matter. I can also give that time to my spouse either when we are together or when we are apart. Each of us needs time for ourselves, alone time, so that we can be a better spouse. I will give the one I love the gift of time off from being with me daily, weekly, monthly or spontaneously.

> *Today I will read or give my*
> *spouse time to read.*

Old Love

Don't you wonder how they did it? Your parents and mine, they lived together for more than fifty years. We are so fortunate to have witnessed their relationships. We saw that they were still separate people building a relationship to the end. Life wasn't boring to them and they weren't boring to each other even after all those years. We have seen it work. It helps one believe it's possible.

Thank you, God, for signs
of your never-ending love.

Calm

Some days I wonder if there is any quiet or calm in this entire world or universe. And then, before I know what is happening, at a time totally unexpected and unplanned for, I find myself gifted with the awesome beauty of quiet, silence and stillness. God, you do hear my prayers! And what a thunderous sound is this silence. It is so intense and concrete that I can hardly take it in. But I will take it in. I will bask in the beauty of this time of stillness. This moment I will listen again to the beating of my heart, to my breathing in and breathing out.

> "One's action ought to come out
> of an achieved stillness; not to
> be a mere rushing on."
>
> (D. H. Lawrence)

Oh God, how beautifully silent
you have made me!

Anger

I think I need to call a time-out in the midst of this fight! I know when I get heated up and in the middle of a conflict that it is important for me to get some space or some sleep and continue the argument when both of us are more rested and refreshed. Never letting the sun set on my anger does not always work for me. Today the best thing for dealing with my anger is to agree that I need to sleep first so I can have the energy and rest needed to talk out this disagreement at a later set time.

God, thank you for helping me know
when to take a time-out and when to speak.

Scratch My Back

I sometimes wonder how many days I could survive without my spouse being there for my itches! In fact I think she causes some of those itches. The door post just doesn't work as good as those fingernails. Oh, how I love to have my back scratched. And no one does it quite like she does.

But now I hear it from our children. "Scratch my back," they cry! Oh God, does everything have to come back to us?

Thanks, God, for good back scratchers!

Scratch My Back II

I'm mad at you. How can you ask me to scratch your back? I'm too angry. But you do have an itch…and so I do it. I start to calm down. I start to remember you and not that horrible person I'm fighting with. It seems to start us talking, as opposed to arguing. We talk about how we feel without the same sarcasm and without the feelings that get hurt with every word. Is that what touching will do? I remember a tool from somewhere that said people who are fighting should have to face each other and hold hands to fight. I can't do that, but I will scratch your back.

God, thank you for the gift of
touch that helps love grow.

Sharing

Sharing all the blessings and gifts I have is good and important to do. I can clean out my drawer or a closet. I can sort and give away possessions, collections and acquisitions because they really aren't mine to hoard anyway. I have so much!

I can share my treasures and walk away from my earthly possessions because God provides. I will set out clothing for the Disabled American Veterans, Association of Retarded Citizens or the community rummage sale. I can do this with regularity for the sake of the kingdom. It is a healthy way of putting Christian charity into practice.

God provides and I can share generously.

Creation

When I see the mountains, the sky and clouds, the grass, rocks and trees, I am filled with the powerful and quiet presence of God.

And who are we that you should keep us in mind, mere mortals that you should care for us? We are the work of your hands. Today I will make a special effort to re-cycle and conserve all that comes in con-tact with my hands, feet and lips. I will say a prayer of gratitude for each moment of beauty.

Thank you, God, for the wonder of creation, the marvel of this planet earth, the immensity of space, of moon and stars.

Sleep

Sleep is a wonderful gift to give myself. Without enough sleep I become irritable, cynical, irrational, depressed and down right obnoxious—just ask my wife, she knows! I can and must take time to get my rest. This time off is absolutely the best thing for my aching bones, my stress and my overeating. This is something major that I can change by just taking a very small action—turning the light and television off! It will do wonders for all those around me and for myself.

When I arrive home this evening, I will take off my street clothes and put on that nice comfortable tee-shirt and shorts, pick up a good book, lay down on my bed and then at 9:00 bless myself with the most extravagant gift of sleep!

O God, bless me with rejuvenating sleep.

Play Together

Today I am going to schedule some play time with you, my love. We could go apple picking, or gather strawberries or blueberries on the farms outside of town. Then we could take a long hike along the nature trail by the river and get to the waterfall by sunset. And if we feel like it, we'll go to a movie later in the evening. I can't wait to be alone together with you for a day.

Thank you, God, for the presence of a kind, caring companion on this walk through life.

☯☯

Patience

So this is how I can grow in being a patient person! This moment, this eternity of waiting, is beyond what I think are my limits. Yet, here I am. It's time to take some greatly needed deep breaths. I can stretch these tense arms, legs and muscles, wiggle my toes, confuse my frown by wrinkling my face, breathe in, breathe out.

I can take this moment to relax, to unwind and say a prayer for safety for my loved one coming to get me at the airport. After all, she would like to be here too, but the realities of rush hour traffic or rush hour parenting has probably hit her hard. No one needs a grouch to greet them when they arrive. I think I'll take another deep breath and stretch once again. And then see if I can't work on those face muscles that create a pleasant greeting. We both will need it (and a hug)!

God, give me patience and a smile.

Supper

Early in our marriage I remember trying to rephrase the question, "What's for supper?" so it didn't sound like it was my spouse's responsibility to have supper on the table for me when I came home. I have learned to say, "What could we have for supper?" or "Do you have any ideas for food today?" Meal planning can be a joint effort. Both of us can shop for food, prepare meals and plan menus.

God, thank you that we are able
to shop, prepare and plan meals.

☙❧

Self-Righteousness

How can people be so judgmental? These are the times when my anger rages! I really have a hard time stomaching such self-righteousness. This must be how my spouse feels when I am on one of my "holier than thou" binges! Oh how we all need to learn to be more loving and let God do the judging. "God is love and those who abide in love, abide in God and God in them."

O God, help me to see the plank in my own eye before I look for a sliver in my spouse's eye. Amen.

God, help us to love and not to judge.

Silence...for a Moment

I've stopped my engine (both my car and my own inner workings) for a moment—stopped moving, driving, pushing, searching, hurting, running, clawing, shouting, screaming, rebelling, clamoring. I have stopped it all—for a moment. God's rain is heard on the roof of my car. I am parked in my prayer place—quiet, alone, still, calm, but God's rain is falling. This time not on deaf ears!

> "Life isn't a matter of milestones,
> but of moments."
>
> (Rose Fitzgerald Kennedy)

I am listening to the silence. Speak, O Lord.

Lonely Trip

When I am out on a business trip, I dream of our future together—just the two of us, traveling to this place or that, taking time to see this absolutely breathtaking part of the country. It sure is lonely now without you, but it is exciting to think about growing old with you, away from job responsibilities, household chores and kids to raise. I'll check out the sites in this area for the two of us to come and enjoy someday. Now that is a most pleasant thought on this lonely trip without you.

I love you and I miss you
on these lonely trips.

Time Out

As a kid, I remember forming the shape of a T with both of my arms so the umpire could see that we needed a time out. That sign might be an important one to bring back and use in this game of married love at times. One of us may have hurt ourselves, or need to catch our breath, or need to check signals with one another before continuing the game of life.

God, help us to not be afraid to
call a time out now and then!

☙❧

Small Things

Today I am going to remember and take note of all of the small things that I do out of love for my spouse and for others. I am going to rejoice in the immensity of the smallest gesture, the smallest act of kindness. And I will notice and be grateful for all of those small little acts of love shown to me as well. I will remember the mustard seed!

"We can do no great things—
only small things with great love."

(Mother Teresa)

*God, thank you for your presence
and power in the smallest of things.*

Wonderful

We have been living our lives in a sense of wonder and amazement as do children, and I hope we will never lose that. It has been a wonderful experience for us in our thirty years of togetherness. Certainly not all joy, but definitely full of wonder! I will take time to make a "wonder" list of our time as a couple. It will go on until we are parted by death—another moment of wonder!

Yes, God, you work wonders!

Westward Ho

Loading up the car for a vacation has always been so exciting for me—new sights to see, places to go, things to do. I guess it's a feeling I knew from childhood when my parents would load up all of us seven kids in the car to head west across South Dakota to see Grandma. And now I wonder how in the world they ever did it! Another suitcase? I thought we had them all in here! Now I'll have to repack again. Whether it is two, eight or twelve, traveling is an adventure.

God, give us a safe and fun trip.

Trains

The summer after our wedding we took three weeks of train travel to visit friends in the West. The rhythm of the rails, the cascading views of God's creation and the comfort of being away from phones and work brought a sense of joy and relaxation to our spirits.

Today, I will take some time away from phones and work too, just to remember our restful time together.

Thank you, God, for trains and travel,
moments and memories.

Signing the Contract

It was our first major purchase, and we were going to give the bank how much interest for how many years!? You have got to be kidding. And then there was the washer and dryer, the car, the second mortgage, etc. And what is so affirming about any of this?

We are still alive and healthy. And just think of the people that we have helped make a good living over the years!

God, help us have a sense of humor!

You Did What?

I can't believe my ears! After all, we have talked about this and you knew how I felt. Yet you still did it! I know that I have chosen to love you in good times and bad, but how bad can it get! I know I need to get control of my anger, and once it has abated a little we will need to talk about this. I think I will tear down that fence that we've needed to take down, or maybe I'll weed the garden, or clean out the garage or take a long walk. Doing something physical helps me work out the anger.

God, help me to deal with my
anger in a way that no one gets hurt.

God Our Creator

Our love is creative. As a couple, we have been and still are co-creators with God of miraculous life, either in the flesh of our flesh, or in the homeless child or in people who need love and hope.

We are father and mother, parent and child, primary care givers who are called to nurture and cuddle one another. We are building the kingdom of God by giving birth to boundless love, day after day. It is never too late for one more holy hug, one more blessed touch or one more gentle word of hope as God's loving partners in creation. Now is the moment.

> *"In the night, in the day, we give*
> *praise to the Trinity, Creator,*
> *Redeemer, Sustainer of Life."*

(R.G. from the song "Praise to the Trinity")

God Our Redeemer

Our love is redeeming for one another and for those with whom we interact. It is the power of the risen Lord that we carry within us as baptized Christians. In the fullness of Jesus we live and work, carrying out his mission for one another and for the world. We are saved by the life, death and resurrection of Jesus, and in that self-giving love we live and love each other. With the power of Jesus we can forgive, heal and love those who have no hope, no wealth, no power.

Jesus, the Christ, redeem
our lives with your love.

God Our Sustainer

Our love is sustaining through the power of the Holy Spirit, for it is the Spirit of God who breathes new life into our often dead bones and sustains our lives. We have been sealed with the gifts of the Spirit so that we can sustain one another and other people in weakness and pain, in crushing tragedy and illness, in times of desperation and loneliness.

Today I will feel the wind on my face or sense the warmth and beauty of flame to remind me of the power of the Spirit within me, within us and within our Christian community.

> "O Great Spirit of Love, bless
> these two now joined as one."

(R.G. from the song "O Great Spirit
of Love")

Come Holy Spirit!

B. C.

Life before children seems very distant and vague. I recall it as romantic and carefree because, after all, I lived twenty-eight years as a single person. My spouse and I lived nine years of courtship after we met one another and two years of marriage before children. Our relationship began before children and it will continue after children.

Thank you, God, for the gift of my spouse before children.

☙❧

W. C.

Life with children is overwhelming. And for many couples without children, life can still be overwhelming. With or without our own children, as couples we are mentors and guides to many young people. Our example as a caring, loving, forgiving couple is the greatest sign we can share with them. As great a gift as children are for us, the gift of each of us for the other is just as great.

Thank you, God, for the gift of my spouse, with or without children.

☺☺

A. C.

Life after children is a long-term dream for us right now. When they all leave "the nest" there will be too much quiet and neatness I am sure, but I think I can get used to it! Our parents too must have rejoiced when the last one left home, and at the same time there must have been some sadness. I will talk with my parents and other couples and ask them how they felt when the kids left. I will remember, though, that there will always be children in our lives as a couple.

Thank you, God, for the gift of my spouse after children.

Let's Eat Out

One of the most enjoyable and relaxing things to do as a couple is to eat out. There are no dishes, food preparation or clean up. Yeah!! Some meals we treat as spouse connecting time—a chance for us to calendar, communicate, update, plan and evaluate. We consider it a business lunch for married couples. We also need other meals together to just be in love with one another.

Thank you, God, for the luxury of eating out with our loved ones.

*May we know you, God, in the
breaking of the bread.*

Sacred Sounds

Lying in bed I would sometimes hear them, my mom and dad, and I knew what they were doing. And here I am with my marriage spouse, making those same sacred sounds of love. And I'm sure our children are hearing us at times, too.

Thank you, God, for the gift of sexual love, for the sounds of pleasure and excitement, for the sounds of joy and wonderful sensations.

ᘓᘔ

Spring

It is so wonderful when the days of spring come. The air feels warm and the breeze is gentle on my skin. Contentment seeps deep into my being. I still have to go here and there and do this and that, but I know the time to enjoy this spring is so short that I must sneak any moment away to delight in it.

"And since to look at things in bloom
Fifty springs are little room..."

(A. E. Housman)

*I want to sneak any moment away from
the bustle of life to delight in you.*

☙❧

Summer

These are the days of vacations, trips, reunions, relaxation and swimming. I can refresh, renew, recuperate and rejuvenate my spirit and soul, but not all at once. The green leaves appear only after days and months of tiny little changes from within the branches and roots—a little warmth here, a little moisture there. I can let God work within my being as well. I can be still and let the warmth of change take root within me, little by little.

Thank you, God, for the
warmth of summer.

Winter

Where have all the flowers, leaves, green grass gone? All is frozen and cold, dreary and gray. And so is my mood. I am so influenced by nature. I can rejoice that I have a warm place to work, play and sleep. I can remember the days when I have been as cold and icy to my loved one as this weather is to me. It's not very enjoyable, is it?

God, help me to break the ice
and warm the chill!

ᙦᙩ

Fall

All the leaves are changing to such stunning colors. Will I look this good when I am in the fall of my life? How colorful am I today, let alone in the future? I can take time to take a walk today with my spouse—holding hands, hugging tight. Our autumn days are before us. How good it is that we can be together as the inevitable changes come.

Thank you, God, for companions
on the journey home.

Forgiveness

"I will never be able to forgive her for what she has done to me! How could anyone be so terrible and hurtful?" Weren't those the words I said a while back? But that hard heart of mine continues to really hurt and I know exactly why. I let my anger out on the pile of wood out back, but the hurt is still there.

God, help me to swallow my pride and speak to my wife again. Help me to forgive her again and again and again! "...as we forgive those who trespass against us." Love is being able to say I forgive you seven times seventy.

"Love is an act of endless forgiveness, a tender look which becomes a habit."

(Peter Ustinov)

Quiet Ride

When the radio is on, my mind focuses on the story and the emotion of the songs pouring out at me, and I'm just barely noticing the neighborhood I pass through. I took a little trip the other evening with the window rolled down and the radio off. It's amazing what I heard and how present I was to the world outside the window. I heard the frogs in the marsh croaking their song, and the children in the neighborhood shouting as they played "night games." I felt the breeze of the evening.

Sometimes in our relationship I think I have the window rolled up and the radio on. It's like I'm passing through, noticing the yield signs and traffic only when I have to. Let this be my day to roll down the window, turn off the radio and really be a part of this neighborhood called marriage.

Today I will be aware…

All Wet

"It's time to take your bath." How many times we have heard that as children. And the bath itself, once taken, was always more than just getting clean. Now that I am grown I have this dream of a large bath tub that I can stretch out in all by myself, or have enough room for my spouse. In the meantime, though, I can squeeze into our little five-foot tub. But every once in a while I need to take time to give myself a bath or give my spouse a bath. I won't just get clean, but I'll really enjoy the soaking.

I can relish in the luxury of wasting time in water. After all, it is where we all began!

Graduate School

The diploma is finally hanging on the wall before me. And it took four years of classes in the midst of work, marriage and children. Can I question my sanity? Yes, I was rather insane to do it, but I am grateful for all that I have learned. I have a much better grasp of the various subjects studied throughout my graduate program but I still can't believe I made it through! Now that we've made it, we can help someone else survive graduate school.

Thank you, God, for the gift to persevere and the understanding of my spouse.

In a Plane

Here I fly in brilliant sky above my ancestors' paths. I don't think they knew that their great-grandchildren would be flying over their homes and graves. I wonder if maybe once or twice they would glance to the clouds above and dream of us future folk. Out the window I see ice and snow and know their graves are there—remnants and treasures of pioneer partners. They labored along through joy and pain, living their lives to the full. When I set foot at my home, I will share some time with my spouse and glance to the sky and wonder about our future folk.

The moments of wonder and the treasure
of a spouse come from you, O God.

'Til Death

I learned a lot about death from Ida. When we bought our house from her, she was moving to a nursing home. She argued about how much we owed her for the shovels she left in the garage, shovels without handles and the handles without shovels. She was angry and bitter, sad and worried. Ida finally let go when she realized that she was going to die. Her life seemed transformed. She became calm and focused. She was happy and knew that many of her worries were just details. "'Til death do us part" reminds me that I only have a little time to devote to my loved one. The reality of death releases me from details so that I can focus on what is important in my life.

God, help me to remember that all I have is a lifetime to share with my loved one.

Bread

Baking bread together is affirming of the goodness of the earth and the joy of teamwork. When this was a completely new adventure for both of us, we simply found a recipe and launched into it. Our time together was precious and fun. Whether the bread was a flop or feast, the process was pure joy. But we had to let go of control and of the fear of failure (both for bread making and for our marriage!).

In our marriage, let's remember that we need to find the child within again. Imagine how that young child would make a marvelous mess of these many textures and love every minute of it! And God is that loving parent watching each moment of our play and providing the basic ingredients.

Enjoy!

☙❧

Down Days

Why are you cast down, my soul? Why groan within me?

It has not been a very good couple of days. In the midst of this I can see no way out— it's like a thick fog. But everything has to begin and end. These down days will end. There is blue sky and sunshine above this fog I am in. I will make it. For now I can try to relax, rest, put my feet up, take a nap. I can go for a long walk, or read a book, or maybe I can find my spouse so I can just be with him or her.

God, help me stay calm.

Massage

Massage therapy is certainly in vogue these days, but I think it has always been the best kept secret of loving couples since Adam and Eve! It is an indispensable ingredient for a loving relationship because it is giving one's own body and energy completely for the comfort and pleasure of another. I think massage clinics are cropping up everywhere today because massage is so desperately missing from so many relationships. Couples need to take the time to rub, touch and massage one another regularly, weekly, if not daily! Every part of the body from head and fingers to legs and toes needs to be caressed and loved, fondled and kissed.

"Lay hands upon us, sister and brother. Tenderly mend, partner and friend. Dance in the circle children and elder. Remember the tales of love without end."

(R.G. from the song "Lay Hands Upon Us")

Giggles

I can't stop smiling when I sit down here to write about it. My sides hurt and I can feel the danger of starting to giggle again just lurking around the corner. We laughed so much I could hardly breathe. There were tears in my eyes and I couldn't stand up, and every time I thought we had stopped it would start all over again. What a great release. I felt like I was six years old and life was fresh and new and without cares when I finally got my breath back. I remember the times this has happened in my life and this was the best because it was with you. Don't forget to invite me the next time you're going to get the giggles!

To the God of giggles, I give praise.

Water Fall/Fountain

It is time to hear the sound of running water, splashing boldly or trickling quietly across rocks. My need for soulful time was realized when I began building our back-yard waterfall and pond. I can use these calming sounds to quiet my spirit, to think of my love. I will rest beside these waters of life and rejuvenation today. They can recall in my memory places and visions of beautiful water falls and fountains that I have experienced.

Thank you, God, for your life-giving waters.

Companions

The source of this word comes from *com*—with—and *panis*—bread. It literally means to be with those who share your bread. Sharing our food at table is such a common, simple, ordinary thing that we do as a couple that we can take it for granted. Then again, in our busy lives some weeks we hardly eat together, let alone sleep together.

Today I will give thanks and be more aware of my spouse as we share a meal. We are companions on the journey.

☯

Good Times and Bad

"I will love you in good times and in bad…" were the words we both said when we spoke our marriage vows to each other. I guess we didn't say that it would be easy, did we? Today is not an easy day to be your spouse. It has been a hurtful day for both of us. I do love you even when I can't stand you! Love is a decision, not just a feeling. Hmmm?

God, you love us and forgive us in good times and in bad. Thanks.

Take Time

The sky is a heavy gray and soft snowflakes are falling. Sounds are muffled and the rest of the world seems far away. I walk in a cocoon of silence seeing small details that would go unnoticed on other days. There are red berries hanging off the stems of yellow-tinged bushes, and the tree branches stand out as black designs against the snow. The quiet beauty enchants me, but I am lonely without you to share this day. When we communicate, let's take time to share these moments and experiences as well as the usual schedules and practicalities of life.

Today, no matter the season,
I will live a quiet, winter day...

Four-Way Stop

I was distracted with other thoughts while driving today and found myself at a four-way stop with no idea whose turn it was to go or if I was holding up traffic. I hesitated, and a driver in another car kindly motioned that it was my turn to proceed. It could have been horns blaring or people angry and shouting but it was just a motion and I was on my way.

I will try to pass on this kindness. I will remember when we meet each other that you might be distracted, and instead of greeting that with impatience which might get us back on the road in anger, I will try to give a helpful gesture or comment that will get us back on the road to communication.

Let me be God's kindness in the world…

Divorce

I remember being shocked that they were getting a divorce. What chance do the rest of us have of staying together if they are calling it quits? Their marriage looked so good from the outside. They were both so organized and looked like they had it all together. When I don't know how to keep on with this married life, let me put it in the hands of God.

God, show me the way.

Memories

I have moved my inner self to the memory of a summer sunset and dusk on the prairie. The day is nearly over for me. I have had another wonderful meal with my parents at table and I am walking along the road. God has blessed my eyes and entire being with the soft, cool air, quiet breeze and glorious colors of the evening sun. The smell of new mown grass and distant water is deep in my memory.

Thank you, God, for the blessings of this moment captured in the innermost part of my being. My prayers rise like incense, my hands like an evening offering.

May the power of this memory
help me to rise tomorrow refreshed
and ready to serve you.

Money

The root of all evil, the source of all pleasure—just what is this stuff that we fight and argue about? God, help us to keep things in perspective. Money is simply a means of bartering for goods and services. We hear it said that plastic is the future; currency is a thing of the past. It might be, but we will still have fights about money even if it is plastic.

Today we can decide to share some of our money with others who need it more than us. Today we can decide to save a few dollars. Today we can decide to buy less and spend only if we have the cash in hand.

"The necessities were going by
default to save the luxuries until
we hardly knew which were necessities
and which were luxuries."

(Frank Lloyd Wright)

God, give us courage to deal with money!

Sex

This, of course, is the second of the three things that counselors say engaged or married couples seldom, if ever, talk about and often argue about. So, what is there to talk about? Let's just do it! Wrong! We have discovered in our twenty-plus years of sexual intimacy that there is much to talk about. And our loving only gets better with practice. Verbal intercourse makes sexual intercourse more fulfilling.

Today we can talk about what touch we like and don't like, about how we like to be touched and caressed. Today we can take more time with each other and help one another.

Thank you, God, for the joy of caring sex.

Religion

And, of course, this is the third taboo subject for couples! Talking about it will only cause fights and draw sides and no one needs another religious war. Let's just pretend religion and denominations don't exist. Wrong again! They do exist, and my parents spent over fifty years living in an ecumenical marriage. They were secure in their own beliefs and practices and were open to experiencing the other's ways as well. They were a sign of the unity that all Christian churches long to have someday.

So today we can decide to worship at various churches and synagogues, meet other people who are strong, yet open in their religious traditions. We can talk story with our relatives; we can listen to one another. We can start an ecumenical dialogue just between the two of us!

God of unity, be with us.

Words

As children we all sang "sticks and stones may break my bones, but words will never hurt me." It was a good chant that helped us keep our heads up when taunted by other children, but as adults we know that words can hurt us. Words have the power to tear us down or build us up, especially words coming from the ones we love and trust the most.

"Anxiety weighs down the human heart, but a good word cheers it up."

(Proverbs 12:25)

God, help us to be quick with encouraging words and think twice before speaking critical and discouraging ones.

Turmoil

Our life is in turmoil. The end of each difficulty seems to bring the beginning of a new one. There are demands on us from all sides. We can remember that we are loved even when it doesn't feel like it. We can take a nap. We can work in the yard. We can go to a baseball game. We can just keep on living. And we can slowly and gradually step back from the turmoil and realize that we can't accomplish everything today, right now. Together we can make a prioritized list of all the demands and then focus on one or two at a time.

God, help us to find hope in the midst of conflict and division.

God's People

We are God's people—sons and daughters of the One who created all of humanity. Male and female God created us—of many colors, shapes and hues. We are God's people.

Today as I sit and walk amidst the hundreds and thousands of people that have no name to me, I will remember that they are my brothers and sisters and someday I may know them or one of them, by name too. But God knows each of them by name.

What a mighty and incredible
God we have as our Creator.

I'm Sick

You're teaching me a lesson about God today. I know you probably don't feel like you are God's face to me but you are. I feel lousy today. I know it happens to everybody but I don't want it to happen to me! You are being kind and gentle. You say "Take care of yourself. Go on, go back to bed." But I am uncomfortable with all of this. I want to be strong. I don't want to be a burden. I don't want to make your day harder. I want to do things for you. I want to earn your love, but you love me even when I am a burden and that helps me understand God's love.

"Pray that I may have the grace to let you be my servant too."

(Richard Gilliard from the song "Servant Song")

Stained Glass

Each day of our relationship is like one of the little pieces of colored glass that make a beautiful stained glass window. The pieces are dull and bright, rough and smooth, crooked and chipped. They are made of a variety of colors that clash and harmonize, but all together they create a glorious image.

God, help us to tenderly create each new day as a piece of this one-of-a-kind stained glass window.

❦

Hope

"I feel like giving it all up in the midst of this stormy relationship. All we ever do is fight with one another." How often have we thought or said these despairing words? Where is hope in the middle of pain and struggle?

The truth of hope is that it is right there in the midst of the struggle. It is *you*! You are hope. Get some rest, take some deep breaths, set aside some time with the problem in the light of another day, then awake to a new day and journey on.

> *"No one would have crossed the ocean if they could have gotten off the ship in the storm."*

(Anonymous)

God at Work

Some days I wonder how or why I could possibly have decided to live the rest of my life with you. We are so incredibly different, and you just will not change to be like me! Wouldn't this world be in a fix if everyone were like me or all the same?

Okay, God, you win. That is exactly why I committed my life to this person who I can't stand at times. Thanks, God, for making us all unique, different and hard to understand at times. Your Spirit is at work within me and within my spouse.

Go, Spirit, go!